The Epistle to the Colossians

An Expository Outline

Hamilton Smith

Scripture Truth Publications

THE EPISTLE TO THE COLOSSIANS

Original manuscript dated 1933

First published 2009

ISBN: 978-0-901860-90-3 (paperback)

A publication of Scripture Truth

Cover photograph ©iStockphoto.com/iacon (Jeffery Borchert)

Published by Scripture Truth Publications
31-33 Glover Street,
Crewe, Cheshire, CW1 3LD

Scripture Truth is an imprint of Central Bible Hammond Trust, a charitable trust

Typesetting by John Rice
Printed and bound by Lightning Source

FOREWORD

I have had these and other manuscripts by the late Hamilton Smith in my possession for about twenty-five years. It was only recently that I realised that not all of them have been published. I know that some appreciate the writings of this servant of God and therefore I am also making these available.

In the manuscripts, capital letters have been used for words such as Apostle, Epistle, Cross, etc. Unless they begin a sentence I have substituted the lower case. I have also substituted the Roman numerals with the usual numbers to denote the chapters in the scripture references. A few spelling and quotation corrections were necessary. I have added some scripture references because not all today are as familiar with the Bible as Hamilton Smith's generation. Otherwise the text has not been changed.

If any soul is established, edified or encouraged the work will not have been in vain.

D. H.

For I would that ye knew what great conflict I have for you, and for them at Laodicea, and for as many as have not seen my face in the flesh; that their hearts might be comforted, being knit together in love, and unto all riches of the full assurance of understanding, to the acknowledgement of the mystery of God, and of the Father, and of Christ; in whom are hid all the treasures of wisdom and knowledge.

Colossians 2:1-3

THE EPISTLE TO THE COLOSSIANS

CONTENTS

1.
Introductory

CHAPTER 1:1-14

The introductory verses of the epistle open with the salutation of the apostle (1-2). This is followed by his thanksgiving for the fruits of grace seen in the Colossian saints (3-8); and finally the prayer on their behalf (9-14).

THE SALUTATION (1:1-2)

VERSES 1-2

The epistle opens with a beautiful salutation in which Paul speaks of himself as an apostle sent with all the authority of Jesus Christ. All that is said in the epistle can be read, therefore, as a message from Jesus Christ and in accord with the will of God. As so often in the epistles of Paul, Timothy is associated with the apostle.

The Colossian believers are viewed as 'in Christ', and addressed as 'holy', involving separation from the world; as 'faithful', and therefore true to God and the position in which God had set them; and as 'brethren', forming a circle of brotherly communion amongst themselves on earth. As such the apostle desires for them the supply of grace and peace which the saints continually need, and which is ever available from God our Father, and the Lord Jesus Christ.

THE THANKSGIVING (1:3-8)

VERSES 3-4

Following upon the salutation we have the thanksgiving which continually arose from the apostle's heart, when praying for these believers. The apostle speaks first of the Christian qualities in these saints that called forth his thanks. They were marked by faith in Christ Jesus and love to all the saints. Not only had they been drawn in faith to the Lord Jesus as needy sinners, but they walked by faith as dependent saints. The reality of their faith in Christ was proved by their love to the saints. Nor was their love after a human sort which might have attached them simply to certain individuals; it was divine love that went out to 'all saints' because they were such.

VERSE 5

Having set forth the ground on which he can give thanks, the apostle proceeds to state what it is he gives thanks for. He thanks God for the glorious prospect that lies before believers – the hope laid up for them in heaven. He is not thinking of what they are delivered from or the scene they are passing through. He holds out no bright hopes in this world, but he sees in the Colossian saints a company of people who are linked up with heaven. The epistle indicates that, at the moment, they were in danger of having their minds drawn from things above by 'the things on the earth' (chapter 3:2). Nevertheless, the danger of defection in no wise alters the fact that God has laid up a blessed prospect for His people in heaven, and for this the apostle can give thanks.

It is surely of the deepest importance to keep this blessed hope steadily before our souls. Rightly we rejoice in the knowledge that we have been delivered from judgement. But if this is all, when the first joy of relief wanes, we may turn back to the things of earth. Even so the children of Israel sang for joy when they were delivered from Pharaoh, and yet, only too soon, turned back in heart to Egypt. Caleb and Joshua, who did not turn back, were men who had before them the land of Canaan. So with Christians, it is only as our hearts enter into the blessedness of the hope that God has laid up for us in heaven that we shall escape the snares that the devil lays for our feet on earth. Only as we walk in the light of heaven shall we be lifted above this present evil world and sustained in our wilderness journey.

Thus these opening verses present the beautiful picture of a company of saints who are the objects of the present favour of the Father, with His unfailing supplies of grace (2); who have the marks which accompany salvation – 'faith' and 'love' (4); and who have a glorious hope laid up for them in heaven (5).

VERSES 6–8

The apostle passes on to remind these saints of the means by which they had heard of this blessed hope. This leads him to speak of the gospel, for, as one has said, 'the good tidings of grace, had wrapped up in it also good tidings of glory' (J. N. Darby). So we learn in the epistle of Paul to Titus, the appearing of the grace of God leads to the appearing of glory (Titus 2:11-13). The apostle speaks of this gospel as 'the word of the truth' in contrast to the 'enticing words' of men by which they were in danger of being beguiled (2:14). There were those in that day, as in this, who would seek to draw the saints back on to Jewish ground; therefore the apostle reminds them of the universality of the gospel. The grace of God cannot be confined to the Jew; it is for 'all the world'.

Moreover, in that day, the gospel was 'bearing fruit and growing' (N.Tr.). Later in the epistle we shall learn that the saints are to bring forth fruit and grow (1:10); here it is the gospel that brings forth fruit and grows. The saints themselves are the fruit of the gospel; the character of Christ in the saints is the fruit that is to be borne by believers.

The gospel of the grace of God had reached the Colossians through Epaphras, the beloved fellow-bondman of Paul and Timothy, and 'a faithful servant of Jesus Christ' to the Colossian saints. He had brought to the apostle the tidings of the genuine work of God that had been wrought in their midst as manifested by their 'love in the Spirit'.

It is of significance that this is the only reference to the Spirit in the epistle. Seeing that these saints were in danger of being drawn from Christ as their one object, the special purpose of the Spirit in the epistle is to exalt Christ before them. For this reason, it may be, the apostle is led to keep Christ before these saints, and to say little of the Spirit – the One who is here to take of the things of Christ and show them unto us.

THE PRAYER (1:9-14)

The apostle has thanked God for the hope laid up for believers in heaven. The certainty of the end of the journey is not a matter for prayer, but rather a subject for praise. We are, however, still in the world, though not of it, and there is a path to be trodden on our way to heaven. This path, by reason of its difficulties and dangers, draws forth the apostle's prayer.

VERSE 9

He unceasingly prayed that these believers might be filled with 'the full knowledge' of God's will 'in all wisdom and spiritual understanding'.

In many passages the will of God has reference to the eternal counsels of God, as we read, 'Who worketh all things after the counsel of His own will' (Ephesians 1:11). In other passages the reference is to God's will for His people in their daily path (1 Thessalonians 4:3, 1 Peter 2:15, etc.). It is so in this passage where the will of God evidently refers to our practical walk. The discernment of God's will for our path, while calling for a knowledge of God's mind as revealed in the Word, is made to depend upon the spiritual state of the soul, implied in the words 'wisdom and spiritual understanding'. The apostle does not suggest that the full knowledge of His will can be gained by knowing the express commands of God, as under law. Still less can it be gained by the advice of others, though brotherly counsel is not to be despised. 'Wisdom and spiritual understanding' would rather imply, as one has said, 'A perception of what is good and wise in God's sight, apart from its being His express command' (W. Kelly). 'Wisdom' is acquaintance with truth in contrast to the lack of wisdom or intelligence (see Romans 1:14). 'Spiritual understanding' is rather the discernment or spiritual insight that makes a right application of the truth to the particular circumstances.

In the path of God's will mere human wisdom and understanding will not avail. It is 'a path which no fowl knoweth, and which the vulture's eye hath not seen; the lion's whelps have not trodden it, nor the fierce lion passed by it' (Job 28:7-8). No eye so keen in nature as the vulture's; no animal so bold as the lion. But the boldness and long-sightedness of nature are not equal for the path of faith. Singleness of eye that has Christ for its only object will alone give spiritual understanding.

The Colossian saints knew the grace of God that had secured for them a blessed prospect in heaven; but, seeing they were in danger of being turned aside by the 'enticing words' of men, by philosophy and 'vain deceit', it would seem they lacked the full knowledge of God's will.

Verse 10

Now we learn that this divine wisdom has in view a three-fold end. First, that we might 'walk worthy of the Lord unto all pleasing'; secondly, that we might bear fruit; and thirdly, that we might make spiritual growth in the knowledge of God.

It is noticeable that in this passage the fullness of wisdom and spiritual understanding is not that we might *do* great things for the Lord, or that we might *teach and preach* the truth about the Lord, but that, above all other considerations, we might *walk* worthy of the Lord. How far more important than all our service and activities is our spiritual condition and practical walk in the every-day life. It is, therefore, for these things that the apostle prays.

Moreover the apostle does not pray that we may so walk as merely to avoid wickedness, which a natural man might do; but that our walk may be worthy of the Lord. The Lord is the standard for our walk. We are not simply to have before us a walk worthy of our own reputation or position, or of our family, or nation, or even of the saints, but a walk worthy of the Lord.

Again the walk is not only to be worthy of the Lord; it is to be 'unto all pleasing'. It is not simply a walk that is pleasing and agreeable to ourselves or our brethren, but pleasing to the Lord. Of the Lord it is written, 'Even Christ pleased not Himself', on the contrary, He could say, 'I do always those things that please Him' (the Father) (Romans 15:3, John 8:29).

How much that we often say and do, would never be said or done, if we stopped to ask ourselves, 'Is this worthy of the Lord?' 'Is this pleasing to the Lord?' We do well then to set out, day by day, with the prayer that we may 'walk worthy of the Lord unto all pleasing'.

Then the apostle desires that we should be 'bearing fruit in every good work' (N.Tr.). Fruit in the believer is always the expression of the character of Christ. The man of the world can do many good works; but he cannot bear fruit to God in his good works. The believer alone can express something of Christ in his good works; so that in the good works that benefit man there will be fruit for God.

Lastly the apostle desires that we may be 'growing by the true knowledge of God' (N.Tr.). The path that is worthy of the Lord, and in which there is fruit for God will surely be one which leads to spiritual growth by gaining an increased acquaintance with God. This surely is a knowledge of God gained by experience, rather than doctrine, though such knowledge will certainly be in accord with the truth.

It becomes evident from this, and other passages of Scripture, that believers are not left in this world to find their way to heaven as best they can, or to walk according to their own ideas of what is pleasing to God. The pathway that God has marked out for His people is one in which His will is paramount, and not theirs. Clearly this tenth verse shows that His will is that His people should walk worthy of the Lord, bearing fruit – that is displaying the character of Christ – and growing by the knowledge of God.

A walk worthy of the Lord can only be as we 'follow His steps'. Of Him we read, 'Who when He was reviled, reviled not again; when He suffered He threatened not; but committed Himself to Him that judgeth righteously' (1 Peter 2:23). In the presence of wrongs, and the hard, unkind and malicious speeches that may be uttered against us, our concern should be, not to defend ourselves and maintain our rights, but, to express Christ; and in respect of any wrongs, to commit ourselves to Him that judgeth righteously. If we make Christ's interest our great concern, we can trust God to make our concerns His interest. Thus exhibiting Christ we shall bear fruit, and grow in the true knowledge of God. One has said, 'We adorn the doctrine of God our Saviour by manifesting in this world of sin, and in the trying circumstances of daily life, not what flesh is, but what Christ is: our hearts feeding upon His love whilst we lean upon His arm and are guided by His eye...Will He fail us in the hour of need? He lets us come into it just that we may prove how abundant are His resources to make us victors over all the power of the enemy' (J. N. Darby).

Verse 11

We have already seen that to take a path that is worthy of the Lord, in which we bear fruit and grow in the knowledge of God will require divine wisdom and spiritual understanding. Now we learn the further truth that it will call for divine power. Such a path is far beyond any strength that nature possesses. Therefore, the apostle prays that we may be 'strengthened with all power according to the might of His glory' (N.Tr.). The more exalted a person the greater his power. Who then can estimate the might of the glory of Christ who is at the right hand of power? In the epistle to the Ephesians we learn, 'the exceeding greatness of His power to usward'. It has been seen in setting Christ at the right hand of God, above every power that is against us whether in this world or the world to come (Ephesians 1:19-21). If Christ in His path is our pattern, the living Christ in the glory is our strength. This mighty power is at our disposal, not here to make us great preachers or teachers, or prominent as leaders amongst the people of God, but to enable us not only to take the path of well pleasing to the Lord, but also to *endure* in the path with longsuffering and joyfulness. We consider Him in His perfect pathway for our pattern: we look to Him in the glory for power to walk according to the pattern. Thus, in another epistle the apostle can say, 'we all looking on the glory of the Lord with unveiled face are transformed according to the same image from glory to glory' (2 Corinthians 3:18, N.Tr.).

The apostle does not ask for strength to *do* some great deed, or make some great sacrifice, on some special occasion. He asks for strength to *be* in a condition that is worthy of the Lord in the quiet of the every day life. How well we know that it is the daily round that is the real test of the Christian life. There it is we need 'all endurance and longsuffering', combined with 'joyfulness'. 'Longsuffering' can indeed at times be exhibited by the unconverted man; who but the Christian can combine 'longsuffering' with 'joyfulness'.

These terms describe what we are, rather than what we do. Patience has reference more to circumstances; longsuffering to our brethren; and joyfulness to God. Such is the path the Apostle desires for believers; a path that has been marked out for us by Christ, for we read, 'He that saith he abideth in Him, ought himself also so to walk, even as He walked' (1 John 2:6). In His path through this world everything was against Him. At every step He had to meet the contradiction of sinners, the opposition of the religious world, and the weakness and ignorance of His own. Yet in the presence of every kind of trial He never did a single thing for Himself, but only the Father's will, showing perfect goodness and all patience, with longsuffering. Looking on His path we see that which will not be found even in heaven – a perfect path in the midst of evil. Such is the perfect pattern for the believer's path. To tread in any measure the path which has Christ for its pattern, will call for the single eye which has Christ for its object.

VERSE 12

The apostle proceeds to tell us the secret of joyfulness when in circumstances that call for patience and longsuffering. It lies in the knowledge of what the Father has done for us. First, the Father has made us meet to be partakers of the portion of the saints in light. Not only is there a portion laid up for us in heaven, but we are made meet for the portion. We are not only made meet to partake of the privileges of the saints down here, but also to share in their portion in light. So absolute is the efficacy of God's work through Christ that it makes His people meet to stand 'in light' where God dwells in the full light of His unsullied holiness.

The Father has taken us up in all our sins and vileness and made us meet for the light. Self-righteousness may say, 'I am not fit'; but faith looking at Christ risen, can say, 'I am made what He is, and therefore I am meet for the saints in light'. There may be deep exercises in learning this. Endless and tormenting questions may arise, if the heart turns in upon itself, but all these questions will be settled when the soul looks away to Christ risen. Christ is risen and there can be no question as to the risen Christ. He is beyond the sins, beyond the judgement, beyond the death, and beyond the power of Satan that He bore upon the cross. What is true of Christ is true of the believer for whom Christ died. If *actually* risen we could not have a question about being meet for the light. But God tells us that Christ Who died for us, is *actually* risen; and what is true of Him is true of the believer *before God.* Is Christ meet for the light; so are we. The thief was made meet to be with Christ the day he was converted. Paul, at the end of his devoted life was not more meet for heaven than the thief who went to glory the day he was converted; though indeed, he was a great deal more meet to live for Christ in this world of evil.

Verse 13

Secondly, not only are we made meet for the portion of the saints in light, but the Father has delivered us from the authority of darkness, Satan, and his emissaries are 'the rulers of the darkness of this world'. Blinded by Satan, the world in spite of all its civilisation, discoveries and inventions, is in 'darkness' or ignorance of God. The Christian has been delivered from the authority of darkness and brought under another authority, even One who has the great and glorious place and relationship to God as 'the Son of His love' (N.Tr.).

Hereafter Christ will be manifested on earth in His Kingdom as the Son of Man; but this glorious Person under whose sway we are brought is One of Whom the Father can say, 'This is My beloved Son, hear Him'. In coming under the sway of 'the Son of His love' we come under One Who, not only can shelter us from every harm, and provide for every need, but Who can satisfy the heart with His unfailing love. Not only are we made meet for light – the light of God – but we come under the sway of love – the love of the Father revealed in the Son.

VERSE 14

Thirdly we are reminded of the righteous ground on which we have been made meet for light, and translated into the kingdom of love. By Christ's work on the cross everything has been cleared away that stood between us and the blessing, so that we can say, 'In whom we have redemption, even the forgiveness of sins'.

In these verses (12-14), the apostle is no longer giving thanks for qualities found in the Colossian saints, as in verses 4 and 5, but rather expresses thankfulness to the Father for the blessings which are the common portion of all believers. Thus he says, 'made *us* meet', 'delivered *us*', 'translated *us*'; and again, '*we* have redemption'. We have had the apostle's prayer to the Father for our walk and spiritual growth; here he gives thanks for blessings in which we are set by grace. These blessings are not a matter for prayer, but a theme for praise. They set forth the position and relationships in which the believer is set by the Father's grace through the work of Christ. The position and relationships, being the result of Christ's work, must be as perfect as that work. We may grow in the apprehension of them, but in the blessings themselves there can be no growth.

To apprehend this is of the deepest importance, for all proper Christian walk, all service, all testimony to the world, flows from the true knowledge of our settled relationships with God. If this is not firmly held, the earnest soul will seek to walk well to secure the relationship, thus falling into legality. Christ's work secures the blessing, though the enjoyment of the blessing will largely depend upon our walk.

2.
Christ, the Work of Christ and the Mystery

CHAPTER 1:15-29

The Colossian saints were in danger of being drawn away from Christ by philosophy and vain deceit, thus losing the consciousness of the fullness of their resources in Christ the Head, as well as the true relation of the assembly to Christ as His body. To meet these snares the Spirit of God, in this portion of the epistle, seeks to attract our hearts to Christ by unfolding the glories of His Person, the greatness of His work and the glory of the mystery.

THE GLORIES OF THE PERSON OF CHRIST (1:15-19)

VERSES 15-17

Already the apostle has brought before us the Son in relation to the Father, as the One under whose sway believers have been brought; now he sets before us the glories of the Son in relation to God. He is the image of the invisible God. In His essential Deity God is invisible; but in His moral being God has been perfectly made known in the Son become flesh. 'The Only Begotten Son which is in the bosom of the Father, He hath declared Him' (John

1:18). None but a Divine Person is adequate to fully reveal a Divine Person. Not until the Son came into the world could the Father's heart be declared.

Scripture speaks of 'image' and 'likeness'; the difference is that likeness is being like another – having the same traits and features; 'image' gives the thought of representing another, whether like or not. God said, 'Let us make man in our image, after our likeness' (Genesis 1:26). Adam was like God in that he was made sinless; he was also in the image of God, in that he represented God as being the centre of a system over which he was to have dominion. Man is still said to be in the 'image of God' (1 Corinthians 11:7), though, as fallen, he is very unlike God. The Son is never said to be in the *likeness* of the invisible God, for He is God, and to say that He is like God might imply that He is not really God. Nevertheless, the Son is 'the image of the invisible God', the One who in His own Person, perfectly represents God in His character and moral attributes, before the whole universe.

Secondly, there passes before us the glories of the Son in relation to the whole created universe. Having come into creation, the Son is 'the firstborn of all creation' – (N.Tr.). The word 'firstborn' is often used in Scripture, as with ourselves, to signify priority in time – the one that comes first. Scripture also uses the word to signify pre-eminence and dignity. God speaks of Ephraim as 'My firstborn', though historically Manasseh was Joseph's first begotten son (Jeremiah 31:9). Again it is said of David, 'I will make him my firstborn higher than the kings of the earth' (Psalms 89:27). Here the word is used to express pre-eminence of David over the kings of the earth, and thus a figure of Christ. If the Son comes into the creation He must of necessity have pre-eminence in position and dignity above every created being, and in this sense, He is called 'the Firstborn of all creation'.

Moreover, we are told why the Son has thus the supreme place as the Firstborn. 'For by Him were all things created', whether in heaven or on earth; whether seen or beyond the limits of our vision; whether material powers or spiritual powers. Further, not only were all things created by Him, they were also created 'for Him', as equally for the Father. Then we are further guarded against the infidel thoughts of men who may profess to believe in his pre-eminence over creation, and yet say that He, Himself had a beginning; for we are definitely told, 'He is before all things'. This statement tells us in no uncertain terms of the divine and eternal glory of the Son. We are carried back to a time when there was nothing created that has been created, to learn not merely 'He was', but 'He is'. These are words that while they forbid the thought that 'He began' or that 'He was made', plainly tell us of His eternal existence as the Son. Lastly, in relation to creation we are told, 'All things subsist together by Him' (N.Tr.). Not only do created things subsist, but they 'subsist together'. The vast creation is sustained by the Son in all its several parts as one harmonious whole. Men would use what they speak of as the laws of nature to shut the Creator out of His universe; but apart from the sustaining power of the Son all would dissolve into ruin. Doubtless there are laws by which God maintains the universe, for God is a God of order, and possibly amidst all men's changing speculations they may have partially discovered some of these laws. But we may ask if gravity is one of these laws, by which the earth is held in its orbit round the sun, Who is it that sustains gravity? Scripture answers, 'By Him *all things* subsist'.

Thus coming into creation the Son takes the place of supremacy as the firstborn, for all things were created by Him, for Him, and He is before all, and by Him all things subsist.

Verses 18-19

Thirdly, there is brought before us the glories of the Son in relation to the assembly. 'He is the Head of the body, the church'. Here we are carried in thought beyond the earth and beyond death. To be the Head of the church it is not enough that the Son should come into creation and take His place as pre-eminent in the world His hands had made; He must go further, even into death, and become pre-eminent in resurrection, thus to become the beginning of a new creation beyond the power of death. In this new scene He associates with Himself, His assembly.

There is, as we have seen, the pre-eminence that belongs to Him in creation by reason of who He *is:* there is also the pre-eminence that He *has acquired* by reason of the work He has accomplished. Thus in all things He has the pre-eminence – 'For in Him all the fullness of the Godhead was pleased to dwell' (N.Tr.). Very blessedly He revealed the Father; but He did more. He revealed the Godhead – the Father, Son and Holy Ghost, for in Him the 'fulness' dwelt.

THE GLORIES OF THE WORK OF CHRIST (1:20-23)

Verse 20

Having brought before us the glories of the Person of the Son, the apostle passes on to speak of the glories of His work. Even as the glory of His Person is presented first in connection with the creation and then in connection with the assembly so the glory of His work has this double aspect. First His work is seen in relation to creation (20) then as it affects those who form the assembly (21-22).

All creation has been affected by the fall. Sin has defiled the whole universe; and a defiled creation must be unsuited to God. So we read in another scripture, 'the whole creation groaneth and travaileth in pain together until now' (Romans 8:22). It is God's good pleasure to reconcile all things to the Godhead, so that everything being in accord with His mind, He will at last view the vast universe with complacent delight.

To remove the pain and discord of creation it was not enough that the Son should become incarnate. He must go into death. It can only be 'through the blood of His cross' that a ruined creation can be reconciled to God. The blood has been shed and put upon the mercy seat, and thus peace has been made before God. How other-wise could God have righteously borne with a defiled creation since the fall? Nevertheless we wait to see the full application of this work to creation.

Verses 21-22

Apart however from created things, there are those who form the assembly. Created things bear witness to the defiling character of sin; persons are also alienated in their minds by wicked works. In further contrast to created things we learn that believers are already reconciled. The work of Christ has not only removed our sins, but brought us into a condition before God, in which He can view us with complacency, as 'holy and unblameable unreproveable'. This is how we are viewed by the Godhead as in Christ. Alas! in our practical ways we are too often far from being unblameable and unreproveable.

VERSE 23

The truth of reconciliation supposes that we are true believers. A reality that is proved by continuing in the faith. The apostle speaks, not of the individual's faith, but of the common faith – the truth believed. If a man who has professed the truth gives up the common faith, we cannot absolutely pronounce upon the individual faith of his soul. We can however judge of the faith he owns, as to whether it is the truth or not. One has said, 'A person may be sincere in what is wrong or insincere in what is right; but the truth is an unbending standard. If one judged on the ground of an individual's heart, one could never speak at all; for of that who can pronounce but God? If one acts on the ground of the faith, the moment a man goes against the truth, giving up what he professed, we are bound to judge it leaving the question of his heart's faith in God's hands' (W. Kelly).

Seeing that the Colossians were in danger of departing from the truth, the warning is given to continue. If they give up the truth no one would have a right to view them as having part in those who are reconciled. Hence the warning not to be moved from the hope of the gospel. The hope of the gospel is in heaven, in contrast to Israel's hopes that are on earth. There were those who were attempting to beguile these saints from their heavenly hopes by the adoption of asceticism, feasts and ordinances, which connected them with earth. Such teaching was not according to the gospel that they had heard and of which Paul had been made a minister.

THE GLORY OF THE MYSTERY (1:24-29)

Having presented the glory of the Person of Christ and the glory of His work, the apostle now completes the truth by presenting the glory of the mystery. The glory and the pre-eminence of the Person of Christ has been presented first in connection with creation and then in relation to the assembly. The glory of His work has also been presented in connection with these two spheres – creation and the assembly. Now the apostle presents the ministry of the truth in this double aspect – first, the ministry of the gospel to 'the whole creation which is under heaven' (N.Tr.); secondly, the ministry of the mystery to the saints.

Verse 24

The ministry of the truth of the mystery had brought the apostle into prison; and in connection with this great truth, he filled up what was behind of the afflictions of Christ and completed the word of God. The truth of the assembly, more than any other truth, exposed the apostle to persecution and suffering, especially from the Jew. The truth that set aside the religion of the Jew and the philosophy of the Gentile – that paid no respect to the flesh in either and proclaimed grace to all – was abhorrent to both. This hatred found its expression in persecution and a prison.

Christ had, indeed, in His great love suffered on the cross for the church. The apostle in his love for the assembly had suffered for *proclaiming the truth of the mystery*. However great and perfect the atoning sufferings of Christ, it was no part of His service of love to publicly proclaim the truth of the mystery. This awaited His new place in the glory and the coming of the Spirit. Then the apostle takes up this service of love, with the sufferings entailed, and thus fills up that which is behind of the sufferings of Christ.

25

VERSE 25

Moreover, the truth of the mystery completes the great circle of subjects comprised in the word of God. This entirely excludes any other subjects that men may seek to introduce as truth or development of truth. One has said, 'The circle of truths which God had to treat in order to reveal to us the glory of Christ and to give us complete instruction according to His wisdom, is entire, when the doctrine of the assembly is revealed' (J. N. Darby).

VERSE 26

This great truth – the assembly composed of believers taken from Jews and Gentiles and formed into one body, united to Christ as a glorified Man, to form a heavenly company – has been hid from ages and generations. It was unknown through all the past dispensations, and unrevealed to the generations of God's people, or even to angelic hosts. When God was dealing with Jews and Gentiles as such, how could a truth be revealed that sets aside both to form a new and heavenly company?

VERSE 27

Now it is manifested to saints, to whom God would make known not only the mystery, or the glory of the mystery, but 'the riches of the glory of this mystery'. The apostle writing to those who were called from among the Gentiles, specially presses that it is made known among the Gentiles and then emphasises the side of the truth so needed by these Gentile believers, that the mystery involves the great truth, 'Christ in you the hope of glory'.

It is true that the mystery also involves the great truth that the saints are represented in Christ – the Head; but the truth that Christ dwells in the hearts of the saints, and that His character is to be seen in them, was the truth most needed by the Colossian saints to meet their dangers. This great truth is the hope of glory, where Christ will be so perfectly displayed in His people, as we read, 'He shall come to be glorified in His saints, and to be admired in all them that believe' (2 Thessalonians 1:10).

It is important to keep clearly before our souls the two great aspects of the mystery as unfolded in the epistles to the Ephesians and Colossians. First, it is the purpose of God that in the church there should be a company of saints in heaven who share the exaltation and acceptance of Christ – the Head. This is developed in the epistle to the Ephesians (Ephesians 2:6, 3:6). Secondly, it is the purpose of God that the character and moral beauty of Christ – the Head, should be displayed in the Church – His body, *now on earth*, as well as in the coming glory. This is the great truth developed in the epistle to the Colossians (Colossians 1:26-27).

VERSES 28-29

In the meantime Paul preached Christ, warned and taught every man, to the end that each saint might reflect Christ and thus be 'perfect in Christ', an expression which implies a full grown Christian.

3.
The Snares that
Beset the Assembly

CHAPTER 2:1-19

In the first chapter the apostle has unfolded the glories of Christ and referred to the glory of the mystery – Christ in the saints 'the hope of glory'. These are the two great themes of the epistle: first, the fullness of our resources *in Christ* the Head of the church: secondly, Christ *in the saints*, actually in the coming day of glory and morally in their passage through time.

In the second chapter the apostle gives us warnings and instructions. He warns us against the different ways in which the devil seeks to draw the saints away from Christ. He instructs us as to the provision that God has made in order that, on the one hand, we may be preserved from these snares and on the other hand, express Christ in our lives.

THE SOUL EXERCISES OF THE APOSTLE (2:1-3)
VERSES 1-3

The introductory verses disclose to us the deep exercises of the apostle's soul. He saw clearly that the enemy was seeking to turn the assemblies at Colosse and Laodicea from Christ, and that unless they were established in the great truth of the mystery of God they would be carried away by these evil devices.

It is instructive to notice the character of his exercises. In the first place he was deeply anxious that the saints should be found in *a right spiritual condition*. Instead of being depressed by the attacks of the enemy, he desires that they might be comforted, or 'encouraged'. Instead of being thrown into strife and contention by the devices of men, he desires that they may present a united front to the enemy by being 'knit together in love'. It would be very difficult for the enemy to gain a footing in a company of saints who were knit together in love.

Moreover, he is anxious for this right spiritual condition, not here in view of Christian service, however important that is, but in order that they may have a true understanding of *spiritual truth*. It is only as the assembly is in a right condition – united in love – that it can grow in the knowledge of the truth. Evidently, while there was much in the Colossian assembly for which the apostle can give thanks, they were defective in the truth of the mystery of God and thus were in danger of being carried away by the enticing words of men. Therefore the apostle desired that believers might enter into the riches of the truth of the mystery; that they might have the full assurance of understanding that comes from the full knowledge of the mystery of God. This great truth tells believers that they are taken out from the Jews and the Gentiles to be united to one another and to Christ in glory by the Spirit, thus forming a new company that is beyond the reach of death, above the power of the enemy, that is in the world but not of it, that is passing through time but belongs to eternity, that is formed on earth but destined for heaven. Men, with their science and philosophy may lay claim to heights of wisdom and knowledge, but in the mystery of God there is found all the treasures of wisdom and knowledge.

Moreover, the apostle desires that the saints may enter into the truth of the mystery in order that they may escape the snares of the enemy, for he immediately adds, *'This I say, lest any man should beguile you'*. Thus he desires a right spiritual condition that we may be able to understand the spiritual truth of the mystery and thus escape spiritual wickedness.

Having expressed the deep exercises of his heart, the apostle passes on to expose the different wiles of the enemy and to instruct us how to escape being beguiled and enticed away from Christ. There are four great dangers against which we are warned: first, enticing words (verse 4); secondly, rationalism (verse 8); thirdly, ritualism (verse 16); and finally, superstition (verse 18).

It will be noticed that none of these evils are the gross things of the world, but rather things that would appeal to the intellect, and the religious side of man's nature, therefore things that are a special snare to the Christian.

ENTICING WORDS (2:4-7)

VERSE 4

The first warning is 'that no one may delude you by persuasive speech' (N.Tr.). This is a warning against error presented in an attractive form by the aid of human eloquence, or by being presented in Christian terms mixed with a measure of truth. Never was this warning more needed than in our day when the world is flooded with popular religious books, containing the deadliest error, expressed in choice language, hidden under attractive sentiments and presented with a veneer of Christianity.

VERSE 5

The apostle was the more anxious for the Colossian saints inasmuch as he could rejoice over them, seeing they were an orderly company, steadfast in their faith in Christ. Nevertheless he felt that unless such enter into the knowledge of the mystery of God they will not be able to stand against the wiles of the enemy. While we gladly own that as sinners we are saved by grace, we have to admit how slow we are to recognise the further great truth that, as saints, we are united to Christ in heaven, Who is the Head of the body, the church, and the centre of that vast new creation according to the eternal counsels of God.

Knowing only the grace of God that brings salvation and failing to enter into the counsels of God for the glory of Christ and the blessing of the saints, the vast bulk of Christians have fallen a prey to the snares of which the apostle speaks.

VERSE 6

However much the enticing words of men might seem to open before us a vista of larger blessing, deeper knowledge and greater usefulness, the effect would be to lead souls away from Christ. At once therefore, the apostle turns our thoughts to Christ. He exhorts us that, having received Christ as our Saviour and Lord, we should walk 'in Him'. We are to walk in dependence upon Him, guided and kept from every snare by the grace and wisdom in Him.

VERSE 7

Moreover if we are rooted in Him as the source of all our blessing, let us seek to be built up and established in our souls in the truth in Him, and thus assured or 'confirmed in the faith'. This confirmation in the faith is the result of holding to the truth as we have been taught in the apostolic teachings. That which we have been taught in Scripture is not to be held half-heartedly. We should seek to abound in the truth with thanksgiving.

Alas! too often saints show how little they are confirmed in the faith, as they have been taught in apostolic writings, by lightly abandoning all they have professed to believe under the enticing words of some leader. How needed the warning, 'Lest *any man*', whatever his gift or sincerity 'beguile you with enticing words'. Whatever we hear, come from whomsoever it may, we are only safe as we test it by 'the faith' as we have 'been taught' in the Word of God.

RATIONALISM (2:8-15)

VERSE 8

In the eighth verse the apostle warns us against a second great snare – the snare of rationalism, or the effort to explain all things by human reason, in order to exclude revelation. The apostle says, 'See that there be no one who shall lead you away as a prey through philosophy and vain deceit' (N.Tr.). Philosophy is the love of wisdom, but the wisdom of man, by which man seeks to search out and explain all things under the sun. Alas! human wisdom leaves out God and leads to 'vain deceits' such as evolution which would fain have a universe without God and modernism which would have a form of Christianity without the Christ of God and the atonement of the Bible.

The apostle meets this snare of philosophy with a threefold condemnation. First he says, it is 'after the teaching of men' rather than the revelation of God. For this reason it shuts out faith. The teaching of man is never faith. To receive statements because men make them, even if the statements are true, is not faith. 'Faith is the reception of a divine testimony by the soul' (J. N. Darby).

Secondly, philosophy is according to the elements of the world and therefore can be appreciated by the world. Being appreciated by the world it leaves its votaries in the world. In contrast to philosophy, Christianity calls a people out of the world for heaven.

Thirdly, philosophy is 'not after Christ'. It leads to speculation: it never leads to Christ. For this reason, apart from every other consideration, philosophy stands condemned by Christianity which is marked by faith, draws people out of the world and gathers them to Christ.

Verse 9

Having warned us of this snare the apostle at once brings before us the great positive truths that would preserve us from being turned aside by the emptiness of human wisdom. First, he turns us to Christ – 'In Him dwells all the fullness of the Godhead bodily'. Instead of the misty speculations of men, we have God perfectly revealed in all His fulness in Christ. There is not a single attribute of the Godhead that is lacking in Christ. Moreover, it is in Him 'bodily'. Christ has taken a body and become manifest in flesh, so that the fulness of the Godhead could be presented in a way that can be known by the most simple of men. It may require a giant intellect to understand even the terms in which philosophy struggles to express its speculations; simple fishermen of Galilee can see the fulness of God in Christ and thus enter into truths that lie outside the comprehension of the greatest natural intellect. One has said, 'To faith which saw through the veil of His humiliation when here, there was not a trait in His character, an act in His conduct, or an expression of the feeling of His heart going out to the misery around Him, that was not the revelation of the Godhead' (J. N. Darby).

VERSE 10

Secondly, the apostle says, 'Ye are complete in Him, which is the Head of all principality and power'. Not only is God fully revealed to us in Christ, but believers are fully presented before God in Him. All the blessing that God has purposed for believers, and that Christ's work has secured for believers, is set forth in Christ, Himself, in His place in the glory above every principality and power. Our portion and position as set forth in Christ is complete. All the philosophy and teaching of men can add nothing to the fulness of the Godhead revealed in Christ or to the completeness of the believer's portion as set forth in Christ.

What is the *righteousness* we have? It is seen in Christ to be a suitability to God's holy nature so complete that it makes us meet to be partakers of the portion of the saints in light, even as Christ is in the light. What is the *life* we have? Christ in the glory is our life: it is set forth in Him. What is the *relationship* into which we are brought? It is set forth in Christ; His Father is our Father and His God our God. What is the *glory* that is secured for us at the end of our journey? It is set forth in Christ. The glory which He has as Man has been given to us. We are complete in Him.

VERSE 11

Having stated the great truth of the fulness of our blessing as set forth in Christ, the apostle proceeds to show the way God has wrought to meet and deliver the believer from all evil within and every enemy without, in order to bring us into this wonderful place of blessing in Christ. He passes before us this great work of God by referring to circumcision, burial, resurrection and quickening.

Circumcision, or the cutting off of the flesh, tells us that in the death of Christ the flesh, with all its evil, has been put off in God's sight. This is something that has been done by God without the intervention of man. It is no question of attainment or Christian experience, though it surely has to be realised and involves experience in its realisation by the believer. For if we own the flesh has been dealt with and condemned at the cross it must be a settled thing with us that the flesh is not to rule in our lives.

VERSE 12

From circumcision the apostle passes on to speak of *baptism* setting forth the great truth that we have been buried with Christ in order that the 'old man' may go out of sight. It sets forth entire separation from the 'old man' – that life with all the characteristics that marked us as natural men. Abraham says: 'Let me bury my dead out of my sight' (Genesis 23:4). That which is dead is to be out of sight. If true to our baptism it would be difficult for the world, or the saints, to tell what manner of men we were before our conversion. The 'old man' that has been crucified with Christ would be out of sight. In chapter 1 we are exhorted to 'walk worthy of the Lord, unto all pleasing'. We are to walk in the sight of the Lord seeking His approval, not seeking to be prominent before men or courting the approval of the world. Thus keeping ourselves out of sight, we should become true witnesses to Christ.

From baptism the apostle passes on to refer to *resurrection*. Baptism separates us from the world, and the man that lived in the world; resurrection brings us into the light of another world. God has raised Christ from among the dead and through faith we know that we are made companions of Christ risen and that if the world is closed behind us heaven is open before us (chapter 3:1-4).

Verses 13-15

Moreover believers are *quickened.* There is a positive work of God in the soul whereby believers are made alive with Christ in a life that is free from sin and death. The body is not yet quickened; for that we wait; but we have a life which enables us to enjoy things above and walk in communion with Christ on our way to heaven.

We thus learn that all that is in us that would hinder our living the life of Christ has been dealt with. The flesh has been condemned by the circumcision of Christ in death; the old man has been buried with Him. Heavenly things come into view by His resurrection and we are quickened with a new life that can enter into and enjoy the heavenly things.

Further, we learn that not only *the evil within* has been dealt with, but every opposing power *without* has been met. As to our sins, they have been forgiven. As to the ordinances of the law, that made demands upon us that we could not meet and required a righteousness that we could not supply, we are delivered from them by the cross. Every spiritual power against us has been triumphed over.

Ritualism (2:16-17)
Verses 16-17

In the following verses the apostle warns us against a third great snare to which the saints are exposed – the Judaising evil. In that day there were those who professed to add to the Christian life by the insistence of Jewish ordinances as to what we eat and drink, and the observance of certain days as holy days such as the new moon and the Sabbath. This snare to which the Colossian saints were exposed has developed into the ritualism of our day. With one verse it is condemned by God as a return to the shadows of a past dispensation. In those days the ordinances of Judaism prefigured the substantial realities found alone in Christ. Alas! Christendom has fallen into this snare; and in turning back to the shadows has largely lost the substance.

SUPERSTITION (2:18-19)

VERSES 18-19

Finally in verses 18 and 19 we are warned against a fourth snare – the worshipping of angels and the intrusion into things we have not seen. This is the superstition of the flesh that loves to pry into the unseen and dabble with the unknown. It might have the appearance of humility that is willing to submit to spiritual beings; in reality it is only flesh indulging its own will. It has been truly said of the angels, 'They have to do with us, but not we with them. Our business is with God' (W. Kelly).

The apostle exposes this evil as being the pride of a fleshly mind pretending to penetrate into the secrets of heaven. Moreover, he warns us that it involves the setting aside of Christ, the Head of His body. To bring angels or any other creature, whether the virgin or saints, between our souls and Christ is to deny our direct union with Christ. He is the Head of all principality and power and as Head to the body He directly ministers all spiritual nourishment through the spiritual help supplied by the members of the body. Thus spiritual growth of the soul is maintained and the body of Christ increases with the increase of God, apart altogether from angelic ministry, which in Scripture is always connected with the guardian care of the natural body.

The apostle has thus passed before us four different snares which make little appeal to gross carnal flesh, but are very attractive to religious flesh. One thing marks all these snares; they do not lead to Christ.

Error wrapped up in enticing words beguiles souls from the steadfastness of their faith in Christ (verses 4-5).

Rationalism, with its philosophy and vain deceit, after the teaching of men, is 'not after Christ' (verse 8).

Ritualism, with its ritual and feast days, occupies with the shadows and not Christ (verse 17).

Superstition, with its intrusion into things unseen, sets aside Christ, the Head (verses 18-19).

Enticing words may easily play upon our ignorance: rationalism may appeal to the intellect, ritualism to the emotions and superstition to the imagination; but none of these things will reveal Christ to the soul, or form Christ in our lives. They do not lead to Christ.

To meet all these evils and preserve us from them, the apostle presents Christ. Having received Christ, He is the power for our walk (verse 6); we have everything *in Him* (verse 9); we are identified *with Him* (verses 11-13); we derive all nourishment *from Him* (verse 19).

4.
The Believer's Death and Resurrection with Christ

CHAPTER 2:20 – 3:11

In the preceding section of the epistle we have been warned against the special dangers to which the Christian assembly is exposed. With verse 20 of chapter 2 we pass to the hortatory part of the epistle in which we are exhorted to apply, in our practical lives, the great truths that as believers we have died and are risen with Christ.

In the practical application of these truths to the life and walk of the believer there will be found on the one hand, salvation from the dangers of which the apostle has been speaking; and on the other hand, preparation for the setting forth of Christ characteristically in the saints, of which he speaks in the following division of the epistle (Chapter 3:12 – 4:6).

THE PRACTICAL EFFECT OF BEING DEAD WITH CHRIST (2:20-23)
VERSE 20

The first exhortations are based on the great truth that believers have died with Christ to the elements of the world. The immediate words of the apostle, as well as the general tenor of the epistle, clearly indicate that 'the elements of the world' are the religious ordinances invented by men or borrowed from Judaism.

The apostle has been speaking of the different snares by which the enemy would seek to draw our souls from Christ. As we have seen, these snares are all of a religious and intellectual character; therefore, in this passage the great fact is pressed that if we have died with Christ it is not only to the gross things of the flesh, but to the religion of the world. Very plainly, the apostle's statements expose and condemn this worldly religion.

First, he shows it is a form of religion entirely adapted to men 'living in the world'. The religion of heathendom, of corrupt Judaism, as also that of corrupt Christendom, suits the world, can be carried out by the world, and leaves men living in the world. Thus it stands condemned by the Word of God, for Christianity takes the believer out of the world by death with Christ.

Secondly, the religion of the world is a religion of '*ordinances*', or human regulations to which the natural man can submit. Such ordinances call for no work of God in the conscience or heart and raise no question of new birth or conversion.

Thirdly, these ordinances consist of *abstention* from certain material things on certain days which men count holy, such as new moons and Sabbath days. They can be summed up by the negative formula, 'Touch not; taste not; handle not'. The soul is thus occupied with material things which perish with the handling. A religion that consists only of obedience to such ordinances must of necessity perish when the things of which it consists perish. Faith puts the believer in touch with spiritual and unseen things that are eternal in the heavens.

Fourthly, we are told that this religion of ordinances is 'after the commandments and doctrines of men'. It is not of God's appointment or according to the teaching of Scripture.

Fifthly, these ordinances of men have indeed in the eyes of the world an appearance of wisdom; for it seems wise to avoid certain things which men are liable to abuse and if abused are harmful to the body.

Sixthly, these ordinances leading to asceticism and 'harsh treatment of the body' (N.Tr.), would appear to show a willingness to worship God while humbling and denying oneself and thus appear exceedingly meritorious in the eyes of the natural man.

Seventhly, such religion stands wholly condemned by God as simply 'satisfying the flesh'. Instead of setting aside the flesh as worthless, it recognises the flesh and panders to its pride. To deny the body certain food on certain set days and treat the body harshly, gratifies the flesh with the feeling of having acted in a praiseworthy manner.

Thus a religion of trust in ordinances, while appealing to a man 'living in the world', is wholly inconsistent for the believer who accepts the great truth that he has died with Christ. For such a one to turn back to a religion of ordinances is practically to deny that he has died with Christ and once again take his place as living in the world.

THE PRACTICAL EFFECT OF BEING RISEN WITH CHRIST (3:1-11)

Having warned us against the religion of the world which we have left behind by death with Christ, the apostle now exhorts to enter into the positive blessings which form the portion of those who are risen with Christ.

The exhortations are connected first with the new world of blessing opened to the believer (verses 1-2); then the new life (verses 3-7); and lastly the new man (verses 8-11).

VERSES 1-2

First the apostle speaks of *the new sphere in contrast to the old*. It is clear when Christ was raised from the dead that death had no more dominion over Him, and the believer being risen with Christ, is free from death as the penalty of sin. There is, however, the further great truth set forth in Christ risen, namely that a new scene with new relationships is opened to the believer. As the risen Man Christ could say to Mary, 'Touch Me not for I am not yet ascended to My Father: but go tell My brethren, I ascend to My Father, and your Father; and to My God, and your God'. After His resurrection the world saw Him no more and His own were to know Him no more after the flesh, but in connection with the Father and His new position in heaven. The believer though having to do with the life here and its relationships, while passing through time, is as risen with Christ, brought into new relationships in connection with the scene above where Christ has gone.

We are exhorted, then, to 'seek those things which are above, where Christ sitteth at the right hand of God'. In this passage the things which are above are set in contrast to 'things on the earth'. This world is occupied with vast schemes through which man seeks, by his own will and power, to improve the condition of the world and bring in a millennium without God or Christ. Looking above, we see it is the purpose of God to bring in a universe of bliss through Christ, and of which Christ will be the Head and Centre. God has given assurance of the accomplishment of His purpose by exalting the One whom men have crucified to His own right hand. Christ on the cross is the clear witness to the failure of all men's schemes: Christ in the glory, at the right hand of God, is the sure token that God will accomplish His purposes. The things which are above are all those things which depend upon Christ at the right hand of God and which God has purposed for the glory of Christ and the blessing of man. It is on these things we are to set our minds and not on the passing things of earth.

The passage clearly indicates that above there is rest where toil shall be no more, for Christ *sitteth* at the right hand of God. Moreover there is power there, which can sustain the whole universe of bliss, for Christ is in the place of power – the right hand of God. Then does not Psalm 16 tell us that at God's right hand there is *fulness of joy* and *pleasures for evermore*? Joys there may be on earth, but the fulness of joy is at God's right hand. On earth the joy runs out, in heaven it is full. On earth the pleasures are but for a season, in heaven they are for evermore. Are not these some of the things that are above, on which we are exhorted to set our minds, in place of having them set on things on the earth? The apostle does not say things that are in the world, but things that are on the earth. Worldly things may include many things that are absolutely evil and for the mind to dwell on such things would be defiling. Earthly things include natural things and natural relationships, which in their place are not wrong, and yet if our minds are over occupied with them they will spoil our taste for heavenly things.

VERSES 3-4

Secondly the apostle speaks of *the new life in contrast to the old*. In the first two verses of the chapter there is opened up to us an entirely new scene – the resurrection sphere – and everything in that fair scene is beyond the reach of death. The things of earth, however right in themselves, are subject to death and the limitations of time. The Christian is not only set in relation to this new scene but he possesses a new life capable of the enjoyment of heavenly scenes and eternal relations. Of this new life the apostle now speaks, for how can we set our minds on things above apart from a life that can appreciate these things?

The life of the world consists in the enjoyment of the things of the world, such as they are. Christ, who is the believer's life is hidden from the gaze of the world and hence the world cannot see the source and spring of the Christian life. Christ can be said to be that life for, in Christ in glory, we see the setting forth of the believer's life in its own proper sphere. This life will be manifested in all its blessedness when Christ appears and we appear with Him in glory. It will then be seen what sustained the believer in life as he passed through the world during the absence of Christ.

VERSES 5-7

Having spoken of the Christian life, the apostle refers in contrast to the things which form the life of the world. Already he has said we are dead to the religion of the world; now he would have us apply death to the activities of the flesh in us. We are to cut off that in ourselves which would link us with the life of the world. If an angel passed through this world he would not be contaminated by the world; there is nothing in the angel that would answer to its seductions. With us there is the flesh – a nature that quickly responds to the attractions of the world and the pleasures of sin. We are therefore exhorted to cut off and refuse the different forms in which the flesh manifests itself – the lusts, covetousness and idolatry of the flesh.

Unless we bridle our desires they will lead us to pursue some particular object with such absorbing interest that the particular thing becomes an idol that shuts out God.

The Christian is called to mortify these members of the flesh. The flesh has been dealt with at the cross: the believer is to deal with the different forms in which that flesh (which is still in him) seeks to manifest itself. The members of which the apostle speaks in this passage can hardly refer to the members of the body. So far from mortifying these members of our bodies, we are told in Romans 6, to yield our members as instruments unto God. The members here would seem to be all these unholy things by which the flesh expresses itself; even as the actual members of the body are the instruments for the service of the body.

It is for the indulgence of these members of the flesh that the wrath of God will come upon the children of disobedience. Refusing the grace of God that would put away their sins they come under the wrath of God that deals with them because of their sins. In times past these believers had walked in these things in which they had found their life. In those days their evil walk was perfectly consistent with their unregenerate life. Now as Christians the apostle exhorts us to walk in consistency with the new life.

VERSES 8-10

Thirdly, from speaking of the new life in contrast to the old, the apostle passes on to speak of *the new man in contrast to the old man*. The evils spoken of in verse 8 are connected with the mind and spirit, rather than with the body. Anger, wrath, malice, blasphemy and vile language, all suppose the mind working in an evil way; whereas the list of sins in verse 5 involve the actual evil deeds connected with the body. Here it is not the evil acts, but the violent and corrupt way in which the flesh expresses itself in committing its evil acts.

All these things are to be put off as forming part of the character of the old man with his deeds, and as wholly inconsistent with the new man. Here, then, the apostle draws the contrast between the old man and the new. These expressions do not refer to particular individuals. They are used to describe different orders of men each having certain characteristics. In ordinary language we speak of 'the black man' and 'the white man', not in reference to any individual but as describing different races of men. Further the expression 'new man' does not mean simply a fresh man, as when we speak of a new man being appointed to fill some position; it implies an order of man that is new in the sense of being entirely different to the old man.

This new man is 'renewed', a word that implies it is daily gaining new strength. This fresh strength is found in the knowledge of the One that has created the new man. As we grow in the knowledge of Christ, so we become like Christ, the One who is the perfect expression of the new order of man. When Christ came into the world there was, under the eye of God, One who morally set forth a new order of man – a heavenly man – with new characteristics. The introduction of the new order of man made the first man, morally, the old man.

The new man is renewed after the image of Him that created Him. The more we have Christ before us – the One in whom the new man is perfectly expressed – the more we become like Christ, and thus practically 'put on the new man' by exhibiting the character of the new man.

VERSE 11

In this new order of man there are no national distinctions such as Greek and Jew: there are no religious distinctions such as circumcision and uncircumcision, nor are there social distinctions between ignorant and learned, slaves and free. The old man may indeed include a variety of men, such as Jews and Gentiles, but all marked by certain evil characteristics. The new man is an order of man in which 'Christ is everything and in all'. Christ is everything as the perfect pattern and object; and Christ is in all to form the character of the new man.

Thus in connection with the resurrection of Christ and the believer being risen with Christ, there is brought before us a new scene – the resurrection sphere in contrast to the earth (verses 1-2); the new life in contrast to the old (verses 3-7); and the new man in contrast to the old man (verses 8-11).

5.
Christk in the Believer

CHAPTER 3:12 – 4:6

We have seen that the great object of the epistle is to present the glories of Christ – the Head of the church, in order that the character of the Head may be expressed in His body.

Having set forth the practical application of the great truths that believers have died and risen with Christ (2:20 – 3:11), the apostle now exhorts us to put on the character of Christ. In the coming glory we shall be perfectly like Christ in a scene where every one is like Christ: now it is the believer's high privilege to express the character of Christ in a world where men are not a bit like Christ. Moreover this new character is not to be exhibited only in some particular circle, on some special occasion, but in every circle in which the Christian may be called to move.

Naturally the apostle first brings before us the expression of the character of Christ in the Christian circle (3:12-17); then the family circle (3:18-21); then the social circle (3:22 – 4:1); and finally the character of Christ is to be expressed towards them that are without (4:2-6).

CHRIST EXPRESSED IN THE CHRISTIAN CIRCLE (3:12-17)
VERSE 12

The apostle bases all his exhortations on the wonderful position in which the believer stands before God. We are 'the elect of God, holy and beloved'. As 'the elect', we are chosen from the world for heavenly blessing according to the purpose of God. As 'holy', we are set apart for God from this present world; as 'beloved', we are cared for by God every step of our journey through this world.

Our walk and practice could never secure this place of privilege before God. Our standing in blessing is wholly the result of the grace of God that has reached us through Christ. While however the walk cannot secure the position of privilege, the position is surely to govern our walk.

Do not these blessings set forth the position of Christ when in this world? Was He not the elect of God – the One chosen from among the people in a very special sense? So too, He was, in the most absolute sense, the Holy One; and on two occasions the voice from heaven said, 'This is My beloved Son'. If by grace we are brought into the same position, it must follow that we should walk as He walked, and exhibit His character.

It is noticeable that in the prayers the teaching and the exhortations of this epistle, there is little or no reference to special gifts and the exercise of public ministry in the service of the Lord. Such themes of deep importance have their place in other epistles: here it is that which is of yet deeper importance – *the spiritual life and character of the Christian* – that is the great theme. What we are is of far greater importance than what we do. We are apt to value one another by our zeal and activity before men, rather than by our spiritual life and character before God. If a believer has gift and ability it is comparatively easy to be zealous and active in public: it calls for greater grace to live Christ in the quiet and comparative privacy of the every day life. To be an energetic worker amongst the Lord's people, or in the world, may make more show; but to be a spiritual man exhibiting the character of Christ in meekness and lowliness, in longsuffering and forbearance, will carry more weight and be of greater value in the sight of God. The ornament of a meek and quiet spirit is in the sight of God of great price (1 Peter 3:4). To be a Martha, with a good deal of bustling activity, is easy; to be a Mary, sitting still at the feet of Jesus, demands a far deeper spirituality. It is not that a quiet spiritual believer will not be active in good works, but the 'life' will precede the 'works' and will ever be his first care. Mary, who was commended by the Lord for choosing 'the good part', was also praised for her 'good work'. But the 'good part' came before 'the good work'.

The result of the good part that Mary chose – the sitting at the feet of Jesus to hear His word – was to form in her the character and graces of Christ. The exhortations that follow very blessedly set forth this character of Christ, marked by grace (verses 12-13); love (verse 14); and peace (verse 15).

VERSES 12-13

The first seven exhortations all set forth the different ways in which the grace of Christ is expressed. *Mercy* is grace to those who in some way may be dependent upon us, and are in special need. *Kindness* does not necessarily imply the meeting of actual need or the conferring of benefits upon one dependent upon us. It is rather ministering to the happiness and comfort of others who may be in no special need. *Lowliness* has respect to oneself; *meekness* has reference to others. Lowliness thinks low thoughts, or no thoughts, of self; meekness gives way to others. These two excellent qualities are illustrated by the word, 'In lowliness of mind let each esteem others better than themselves' (Philippians 2:3). The lowly man makes himself of no reputation; the meek man considers the qualities of others rather than his own.

Longsuffering has reference more to trying circumstances; *forbearing* one another refers to trying people. We rightly speak of a person showing great forbearance in the presence of provocation. This provocation may be general – something that calls for the forbearance of all. There may also be personal wrongs, which would give just cause for complaint by the one wronged. Such personal wrongs call for *forgiveness*. The measure of the forgiveness is to be even as Christ forgave us.

VERSE 14

Then we read, 'To all these things add *love*' (N.Tr.). It is not, as in our Authorised Version, 'Above all these things put on love', as if above all these qualities there is 'love' as a quality apart. Love is to be added to the mercy, the kindness and all the other qualities. All these blessed activities of the new man are to spring from love. If we show mercy or kindness or forbearance or forgiveness, it should be because we love our brother. Love is 'the bond of perfectness'. The apostle is speaking of the new order of man in which alone perfection can be found. In the old order, men are hateful and hating one another; in the new all are bound together in the eternal bonds of love. One has said, 'The links which are riveted in the love of Christ and in labours for Christ, outlive the changes of time and bind the family of God in the mansions of eternity'.

VERSE 15

'Let the *peace of Christ* preside in your hearts' (N.Tr.). In Christ we see the new order of man set forth in perfection. He came down from heaven and could speak of Himself as 'the Son of Man which is in heaven' (John 3:13). He walked amidst earth's unrest, but lived in heaven's calm. We pass through a world where there is no peace. Politically it is a world of wars. Socially, commercially and religiously all is unrest and upheaval. The privilege of the Christian is to pass through it, even as Christ, with the peace and calm of heaven in his heart, whatever the circumstances through which he may be called to pass.

Furthermore the peace is not only to preside in our hearts, but to be enjoyed in the Christian company; for to this we have been 'called in one body'. Oneness of the body requires peace between the members if it is to grow with the increase of God. Further if there is peace in the heart, there will be thankfulness to God. Thus, if marked by grace, love and peace, the beautiful character of Christ will be reproduced in His people.

VERSES 16-17

The character of Christ found in the saints as set forth in verses 12 to 15, prepares for the service of Christ as unfolded in verses 16 and 17. In these verses the apostle speaks of teaching, admonishing, singing, doing and giving thanks. The meaning of verse 16 is a little obscured in our Authorised Version by somewhat defective punctuation. There are three distinct exhortations. First, 'Let the word of Christ dwell in you richly': secondly, 'In all wisdom teaching and admonishing one another': thirdly, 'In psalms and hymns and spiritual songs, singing with grace in your hearts to God' (N.Tr.).

The first exhortation is individual; we are each to be instructed in the mind of Christ. Then, having the mind of Christ for ourselves we are to teach and admonish one another. Here the exhortation does not appear to contemplate public ministry by one specially gifted to teach; but rather teaching and admonishing one another individually, as the outcome of each one having the word of Christ through having sat at His feet and heard His word. The third exhortation gives the proper attitude of praise to God. If we sing to God it should be with grace in our hearts, not simply with melody on our lips.

In verse 17 we pass to 'doing'. Whatsoever we do in word or deed, is to be done in the Name of the Lord Jesus. What a simple but searching rule of life. How beautiful will be the life in which nothing is ever said or done, but what is suitable to that blessed and holy Name. How many questions that perplex us in the daily life, would at once be solved by this simple test, 'Can I do or say this in the Name of the Lord Jesus'?

The closing exhortation is 'Giving thanks unto God the Father by Him'. In the midst of all circumstances we are to give thanks. The Lord, when rejected by Israel could say, 'I thank Thee O Father, Lord of heaven and earth': and Paul could sing in the inner prison, with his feet fast in the stocks. We learn from these exhortations how intimately the character of Christ in the saints, and the practical life they lead, are linked together. The character we put on must affect the life we live, expressed in our words and deeds.

CHRIST EXPRESSED IN THE FAMILY CIRCLE (3:18-21)

In verses 18 to 21 we have practical exhortations in reference to the natural relationships established by God – wives, husbands, children and fathers. Christianity, while introducing into relationships above the relationships of earth, does not set aside the earthly relationships, while we are yet in the body. They were instituted by God, sanctioned by the Lord and are to be respected by the Christian.

Fallen man has abused these relationships: the Christian is instructed how to maintain them according to the mind of God, so that, in the family there may be an expression of the excellencies of Christ – the subjection, the obedience, the love and the grace – that marked His earthly path.

Verse 18

Christian wives are exhorted to own the authority of their husbands by due subjection. This indeed is only fitting in those who profess to submit to the Lord. Being subject 'in the Lord' would give strength to carry out the exhortation, while at the same time, guarding the submission from degenerating into acquiescence in evil.

Verse 19

Husbands are to see that they love their wives and, thus instead of being betrayed into any bitterness, express the character of Christ by using authority in the spirit of love.

Verse 20

Children are to obey their parents in all things, not simply as well pleasing in the family circle, but as well pleasing to the Lord. Walking in obedience they would exhibit something of the beautiful character of Christ, Who, in the days of His flesh was 'subject' to His parents (Luke 2:51).

VERSE 21

Fathers are to beware lest they assert their authority in an arbitrary way and thus estrange the child's affection by any unjust punishment, or dishearten the child by needless fault finding. They are to seek to exhibit that perfect wisdom of Christ, Who knew how to correct His disciples while retaining their affections (Luke 22:24-30).

These exhortations suppose the Christian household, where all right authority is maintained, but under the Lord and therefore exercised in a way that is pleasing to the Lord in a spirit of love.

We approach these special exhortations to the family circle through the exhortations addressed to the Christian circle. If we are right in the Christian circle, if we are seeking things above, if we are mortifying the members of the flesh, if we have practically put off the old man and put on the new, and are thus marked by the grace, love and peace of Christ, we shall be prepared to carry out rightly the relationships of the family circle.

Nevertheless, the flesh is still in us and therefore each one is exhorted in a way that will strengthen against the thing in which each is likely to fail. The flesh in the woman may at times rebel against the authority of the man; she is therefore exhorted to submit. The man may more easily break down in affection than the woman; he is therefore exhorted to love. Children are prone to do their own wills; they are therefore warned to obey. The father may act in an arbitrary way; so is warned not to provoke his children.

How happy the home in which the wife's submission is yielded in the Lord; where the husband's authority is exercised in love; where the children obey to please the Lord; and where the father acts with the wisdom of Christ.

CHRIST EXPRESSED IN THE SOCIAL CIRCLE (3:22 – 4:1)
CHAPTER 3:22 – 4:1

It will be noticed that the first relationships of which the apostle speaks are those which had their existence in the garden of Eden – wife and husband. Then we come to relationships which came into being after the fall – children and parents. Finally we come to relationships of which we hear nothing until after the flood – servants and masters (Genesis 9:25).

Apparently the existence of masters and slaves was not contemplated in the creation order. This being so, it might be thought that Christianity would entirely ignore, if not actually prohibit, such institutions amongst men. This however is not so: Christianity neither sanctions nor condemns slavery, for it is no part of the work of grace to 'set itself to change the state of the world, and of society' (J. N. Darby). Its great purpose is to call a people out of the world to Christ, bringing them into new and heavenly relationships.

Those Christians however, who find themselves in these different social positions are instructed how to act so that while in them, they may express something of the character of Christ.

Christian slaves are to carry out their obedience to their masters, no longer to ingratiate themselves with their masters, or as pleasing themselves or others, but with a heart governed with the desire to please the One of Whom it is written 'even Christ pleased not Himself'. Whatever has to be done, however menial or irksome, is to be done as to the Lord. Thus, though a slave to man, the Christian slave serves the Lord and serving the Lord, will be recompensed by the Lord. In that coming day of recompense, if not in the present, it will be made manifest that with the

Lord there is no respect of persons. He that does wrong, whether master or slave will receive for the wrong that he has done. Masters, then, are to act towards their slaves in the fear of the Lord, knowing that they have a Master in heaven. So doing they will give to their slaves what is just and due.

Chapter 4:2-4

These special exhortations to different individuals are closed by a general exhortation to prayer that applies to all saints. The mere fact of knowing the mind of the Lord for each one in these relationships is not enough. Knowledge of itself is not power. We need to be kept in the dependent attitude of prayer, if we are to carry out the exhortations in practice. We are therefore exhorted to 'Persevere in prayer, watching in it with thanksgiving'. Persevering in prayer would imply, not only turning to God in some special need, but the habitual attitude of dependence upon God. Whatever the difficulty, however prolonged the trial, though the answer may be delayed, we are to 'persevere in prayer'. The prayer is to be accompanied with watching and thanksgiving. The Lord warned His disciples to watch and pray. It is useless to pray in reference to a particular temptation or snare if at the same time we do not watch against it. Prayer without watchfulness becomes mere formality. It may be also, that the watchfulness has reference to the expectation of an answer to the prayer, and in this sense we are to watch for the answer.

Exhorting others to pray led the apostle to feel his own deep need of the prayers of the Lord's people. Hence he asks for their prayers that God would open to him a door of utterance, and that door being opened, that he might be able to unfold the mystery of Christ and to do so in a right manner as he 'ought to speak'.

CHRIST EXPRESSED TOWARDS THOSE WHO ARE WITHOUT (4:5-6)
VERSES 5-6

Finally we are exhorted as to our walk and conversation with those who are without the Christian circle. A right walk will call for wisdom and the readiness to avail ourselves of the opportunities that present themselves to speak for the Lord. Our danger is that we may have wisdom but lack boldness; or that we may manifest great boldness accompanied with little wisdom.

We carry a message of grace, to be expressed in words of grace; at the same time our speech is to be seasoned with the salt of holiness. Thus speaking our grace will not degenerate into lightly passing over sins or our faithfulness into mere hard condemnation of sinners. For this combination of grace and 'salt' we need the wisdom of Christ, Who, not only knew the right answer to give every enquirer or opposer, but how to answer so as to meet the need of each one.

6.
The Closing Salutations

CHAPTER 4:7-18

The salutations with which the epistle closes present a beautiful picture of the Christian love, the mutual interest in one another's circumstances and the tender regard for the spiritual welfare of the Lord's people, that existed in the Christian circle in the days before the church, as a united witness for God, became ruined and the people of God became divided and scattered.

VERSES 7-9

Two brothers in the Lord – Tychicus and Onesimus – were linked together in the service of carrying this letter to the Colossian assembly. Very happily the apostle can speak of Tychicus as, not only a 'brother' but 'a *beloved* brother'; not only as a 'minister' but as 'a *faithful* minister'; and not only a 'servant' but as a *'fellowservant'* with the apostle in the Lord. These Christian traits were so evenly combined in this servant that his love did not hinder his faithfulness, nor his faithfulness preclude his fellowship with others. Onesimus, one of the Colossian saints is also commended as a faithful and beloved brother, though nothing is said to indicate that he took part in public ministry. Probably he was not a gifted brother. Remembering that he was socially a slave, the commendation he receives from Paul would show how thoroughly he answered to the exhortations given for the slave in this epistle.

These two brothers would make known to the Colossian brethren 'all things' in connection with Paul and the Lord's interests at Rome. In order to bring back a report to the apostle, Tychicus would learn their state and at the same time would encourage their hearts by letting them know of the apostle's deep interest in them. Love counted on their interest in the apostle, even as his love desired to know their welfare.

VERSES 10-11

The apostle then mentions three brethren of the circumcision: first, Aristarchus, who at the time of writing was a fellow-prisoner with the apostle; secondly, Mark, the relative of Barnabas, concerning whom they had already received commandments which were not necessary to repeat, nor probably suited for a public letter. It would seem that the Colossian assembly had heard that Mark had once turned back from the work, and coming under the displeasure of the apostle had sailed to Cyprus with his relative Barnabas (Acts 15:37-39). Paul would have them now to know how thoroughly Mark had regained his confidence, by specially commending him for their reception, if he came to them. These two brothers, with Justus, were apparently the only brothers of the circumcision working with the apostle for the kingdom of God, who had been a comfort to him in his imprisonment at Rome.

VERSES 12-13

Already we have learnt, from the early part of the epistle, that Epaphras had laboured amongst the Colossian saints as a faithful minister of Christ. Now we learn that, though no longer with them, he still laboured fervently in prayer for them and the saints in the neighbouring towns of Laodicea and Hierapolis. It would seem that he realised that the enemy was making a definite attack upon these assemblies in order to draw them away from Christ by religious devices. In the presence of this opposition the apostle speaks of Epaphras as 'combating earnestly for you in prayers' (N.Tr.). A wholesome and encouraging reminder that prayer is a powerful weapon in meeting the opposition of the enemy. Moreover, Epaphras not only desired that the efforts of the enemy might be frustrated, but also that the saints might 'stand perfect and complete in all the will of God'. He realised that if full grown Christians and established in the truth according to the will of God, they would be able to stand against every attack of the enemy.

Verse 14

Luke is referred to as 'the beloved physician', proving that his earthly calling as a physician was not incompatible with his yet higher call to ministry as the companion of the apostle in his travels, and as the inspired writer of the Gospel.

The mention of Demas without a word of commendation is ominous in the light of the next and last mention of Demas in the second epistle to Timothy, from which we learn that he had forsaken Paul, having loved this present world. It spoke well for the apostle that he was one with whom no man could continue who loves this present world.

Verses 15-16

Salutations are sent to the brethren at Laodicea and to one whose house was the gathering place of an assembly of

God's people. The apostle apparently saw that the assembly at Laodicea was exposed to the same dangers that were threatening the assembly at Colosse and therefore specially directs that this epistle be read in their midst. From their after history it would seem that they took but little heed to, or soon forgot, the solemn warnings of the epistle against the intrusion of religious flesh which leads the soul away from Christ 'to the satisfying of the flesh' (2:6, 18, 23). So finally it comes to pass that satisfied with themselves they boast in their spiritual riches and can even say they have need of nothing when Christ is outside.

As with the Laodicean assembly, so with Christendom, it has paid little or no heed to the warnings of this epistle, with the result that it has become leavened with modernism, ritualism and superstition. Like the Laodiceans the great mass of professing Christendom while boasting in its wealth and taking the name of Christ, yet deny the glory of His Person, and the efficacy of His work, and so hasten on to the time when they will be spued out of Christ's mouth.

VERSE 17

Apparently Archippus needed a special message to take heed to the ministry he had received in the Lord, in order to fulfil it. How many of us require this same exhortation, seeing that in the presence of many discouragements and much opposition, we may grow weary. Our part is to persevere in any little service the Lord may have entrusted us with, even if at the moment we see but little result.

VERSE 18

The apostle closes the epistle with the usual salutation from his own hand. He reminds them of his bonds, the witness of his love to the Lord and to the saints, which led him to endure imprisonment rather than surrender the truth. Finally he commends them to the grace of God.

OTHER BOOKS BY HAMILTON SMITH
FROM SCRIPTURE TRUTH PUBLICATIONS

"THE LORD IS MY SHEPHERD" AND OTHER PAPERS

ISBN 978-0-901860-06-4; (paperback)

97 pages; July 1987

THE GOSPEL OF MARK: AN EXPOSITORY OUTLINE

ISBN 978-0-901860-69-9; (paperback)

ISBN 978-0-901860-70-5; (hardback)

144 pages; March 2007

THE EPISTLE TO THE ROMANS: AN EXPOSITORY OUTLINE

ISBN 978-0-901860-85-9; (paperback)

196 pages; June 2008

ELIJAH: A PROPHET OF THE LORD

ISBN 978-0-901860-68-2; (paperback)

80 pages; March 2007

ELISHA: THE MAN OF GOD

ISBN 978-0-901860-79-8; (paperback)

92 pages; March 2007

SHORT PAPERS ON THE CHURCH

ISBN 978-0-901860-80-4; (paperback)

96 pages; March 2008

EXTRACTS FROM THE LETTERS OF SAMUEL RUTHERFORD

ISBN 978-0-901860-81-1; (paperback)

96 pages; March 2008

EXTRACTS FROM THE WRITINGS OF WILLIAM GURNALL

  ISBN 978-0-901860-82-8; (paperback)

  100 pages; August 2008

EXTRACTS FROM THE WRITINGS OF THOMAS WATSON

  ISBN 978-0-901860-83-5; (paperback)

  96 pages; April 2009

OTHER BOOKS FROM SCRIPTURE TRUTH PUBLICATIONS

NEW TESTAMENT COMMENTARY SERIES BY F. B. HOLE:

THE GOSPELS AND ACTS

  ISBN 978-0-901860-42-2 (paperback)

  ISBN 978-0-901860-46-0 (hardback)

  392 pages; February 2007

ROMANS AND CORINTHIANS

  ISBN 978-0-901860-43-9 (paperback)

  ISBN 978-0-901860-47-7 (hardback)

  176 pages; February 2007

GALATIANS TO PHILEMON

  ISBN 978-0-901860-44-6 (paperback)

  ISBN 978-0-901860-48-4 (hardback)

  204 pages; February 2007

HEBREWS TO REVELATION

  ISBN 978-0-901860-45-3 (paperback)

  ISBN 978-0-901860-49-1 (hardback)

  304 pages; February 2007

UNDERSTANDING THE OLD TESTAMENT SERIES:

THE GOSPEL IN JOB BY YANNICK FORD
ISBN 978-0-901860-76-7 (paperback)
ISBN 978-0-901860-77-4 (hardback)
112 pages; March 2007

HOW TO OVERCOME BY JOHN T MAWSON
ISBN 978-0-901860-62-0 (paperback)
144 pages; April 2009

DELIVERING GRACE BY JOHN T MAWSON
ISBN 978-0-901860-64-4 (paperback)
ISBN 978-0-901860-78-1 (hardback)
192 pages; March 2007

LESSONS FROM EZRA BY TED MURRAY
ISBN 978-0-901860-75-0 (paperback)
84 pages; March 2007

LESSONS FROM NEHEMIAH BY TED MURRAY
ISBN 978-0-901860-86-6 (paperback)
124 pages; August 2008

UNDERSTANDING CHRISTIANITY SERIES:

SEEK YE FIRST BY JOHN S BLACKBURN
ISBN 978-0-901860-61-3 (paperback)
ISBN 978-0-901860-02-6 (hardback)
136 pages; February 2007

GOD AND RELATIONSHIPS BY COR BRUINS
ISBN 978-0-901860-36-1 (paperback)
108 pages; August 2006

"THE EPISTLE OF CHRIST" EDITED BY F. B. HOLE
ISBN 978-0-901860-73-6 (paperback)
140 pages; March 2008

GOD'S INSPIRATION OF THE SCRIPTURES BY WILLIAM KELLY
ISBN 978-0-901860-51-4 (paperback)
ISBN 978-0-901860-56-9 (hardback)
484 pages; March 2007

LECTURES ON THE CHURCH OF GOD BY WILLIAM KELLY
ISBN 978-0-901860-50-7 (paperback)
244 pages; February 2007

ISBN 978-0-901860-55-2 (hardback)
244 pages; March 2007

UNDERSTANDING THE NEW TESTAMENT SERIES:

PATMOS SPEAKS TODAY BY JOHN WESTON
ISBN 978-0-901860-66-8 (paperback)
88 pages; February 2007

www.ingramcontent.com/pod-product-compliance
Lightning Source LLC
Chambersburg PA
CBHW032215040426
42449CB00005B/599